© 2021 Progressive Casualty Insurance Company.
All rights reserved.

Eleven Letter Press
6300 Wilson Mills Rd
Mayfield, OH
44143, USA

ISBN 9780578992921 (hardcover) | ISBN 9780578992938 (ebook)

To George and Rose,

Thank you for being the parents I always swore I wouldn't become, then became anyway. But then I un-became you and it led me to help others un-become their parents.

Always your son,
Rick, Parenta-Life Coach

A Note From the Author

Being the world's foremost expert in *Parentamorphosis* is not what qualifies me to help you un-become your parents. What qualifies me is that I was a sufferer too. I bought my first home and before I knew it I was extolling the virtues of clover as a high-traffic lawn solution and explaining the difference between watts and lumens to random store patrons.

That's when I knew, I had become my dad.

Through the long and painful journey of un-becoming my father, I realized that if there was any hope for the millions of sufferers out there...that hope was me. The following pages aren't just an easy-to-digest collection of my learnings. It's a lifesaver I'm tossing into the torrid ocean of *Parentamorphosis*. So grab hold. I'm here to save you.

Dr. Rick

-Dr. Rick, Parenta-Life Coach

Table of Contents

01 Socializing

Un-talk Like Your Parents 10
Quick Tip: Giving Directions 18
Telling Stories 20
Things That Don't Need to Be Announced 22
Quick Tip: Unsolicited Parking Help 24
Weather 26

02 Physicality

A Stance at a Glance 30
Is a Noise Necessary? 36
Turning the Page 38
Nap Traps 40
Stretching in Public 48

03 Clothing & Accessories

Footwear 52
Quick Tip: A Need for Knee Braces 62
Transitioning Away from Transition Lenses 64
Quick Tip: Just Because It's Free 66
Should It Fasten? 68
Quick Tip: Wind Pants 76

04 Home

Beware of Beige 80
This Is Not Your Glass 82
Throw These Things Away, Now 84
Quick Tip: Decorative Soap 86
This Is Not Your Thermostat 88
Quick Tip: Aprons Are for Cooking 90

05 Media & Culture

Holding a Cellphone 94
Quick Tip: Tablet Photography 98
Watching TV 100
Quick Tip: Passwords 102
Emojis to Avoid 104
Quick Tip: Plaques 106
How to Take a Selfie 108
Pronouncing Foods 110

01

Socializing

You ever hear yourself say something and think "that's something my Dad would say"? Well, everyone else hears it, too. In this section, we'll have a look at some common yet treacherous missteps.

Un-talk Like Your Parents

When you open your mouth, who's doing the talking? You or your parents?

The exercises in this section will help sharpen your non-parent speaking skills.

LET'S GET TO WORK

SOCIALIZING

SOCIALIZING

What Should You Say?

1 **When you pass a construction worker, what should you say?**

- A) Workin' hard or hardly workin'?
- B) What we got here, box girders?
- C) Smile and nod because you don't know them.
- D) Fine piece of craftsmanship.

2 **When greeting a barista, what should you say?**

- A) Mornin', Chief.
- B) Howdy.
- C) Hidee ho.
- D) Small coffee, please.

SEE HOW YOU DID

Answers: 1: C | 2: D

SOCIALIZING

Charting the Course

The following charts outline parental things you should stop saying in common social situations. Practice using the phrase in the right column instead.

REFERRING TO A FUNNY MOMENT

WHAT YOUR PARENTS SAY	WHAT YOU SHOULD SAY
It was a hoot.	It was funny.
It was a riot.	
I was in stitches.	
We had a good chuckle.	
I laughed and laughed.	

SOCIALIZING

GREETING ADOLESCENTS

WHAT YOUR PARENTS SAY	WHAT YOU SHOULD SAY
Hey, slugger.	Hi.
Hey there, champ.	
How you doing, sport?	
Hey, big guy.	
How you doing, tiger?	

SOCIALIZING

WHEN THE WAITER CLEARS YOUR TABLE

WHAT YOUR PARENTS SAY	WHAT YOU SHOULD SAY
Our compliments to the chef.	
Clean plate club.	
We obviously hated it.	Thank you.
Time for a nap.	
OK, twist my arm. Let's see a dessert menu.	

QUICK TIP

FROM DR. RICK

Giving Directions

You're not a 16th century explorer navigating the seven seas, so let's avoid using north, south, east, and west when giving directions. Stick to the basics like left, right, and straight. Your help shouldn't require a compass or the ability to read the sun.

Telling Stories

Extraneous details do not make a story better. The opposite actually. So let's focus on trimming and get right to the point.

SOCIALIZING

WE SAW THE MOST AMAZING THING YESTERDAY WHEN WE WERE WALKING BY BARBARA'S HOUSE. YOU KNOW THE BEIGE TUDOR WITH THE NICE HARDSCAPING? SHE WAS OUTSIDE WITH HER TWO BOYS, OLIVER AND QUINTON, SO WE STOPPED TO CHAT. QUINTON IS THE ONE WHO GETS EAR INFECTIONS FROM THE POOL, WHICH THEY'VE NEVER BEEN ABLE TO FIGURE OUT. AND HER NEIGHBOR DEBORAH WAS THERE, TOO. YOU KNOW DEBORAH — THE ONE WITH THE LITTLE TERRIER. IT KIND OF LOOKS LIKE THE DOG FROM THE SHOW I LIKE, BUT IT HAS MORE BROWN IN ITS COAT. ANYWAY, WE STOPPED TO TALK, BECAUSE YOU KNOW DEBORAH, SHE'S A TALKER. SO AS WE'RE ALL STANDING THERE, OLIVER, BARBARA'S SON WHO'S BEEN GETTING REALLY INTO TRAINS, LOOKS UP AND POINTS AT A BIG BIRD THAT WAS FLYING BY. SO WE ALL TURN AND WHAT DO YOU KNOW, THERE WAS THIS BEAUTIFUL, MAJESTIC BIRD RIGHT ABOVE US. AND WOULD YOU BELIEVE IT, IT WAS AN EAGLE!

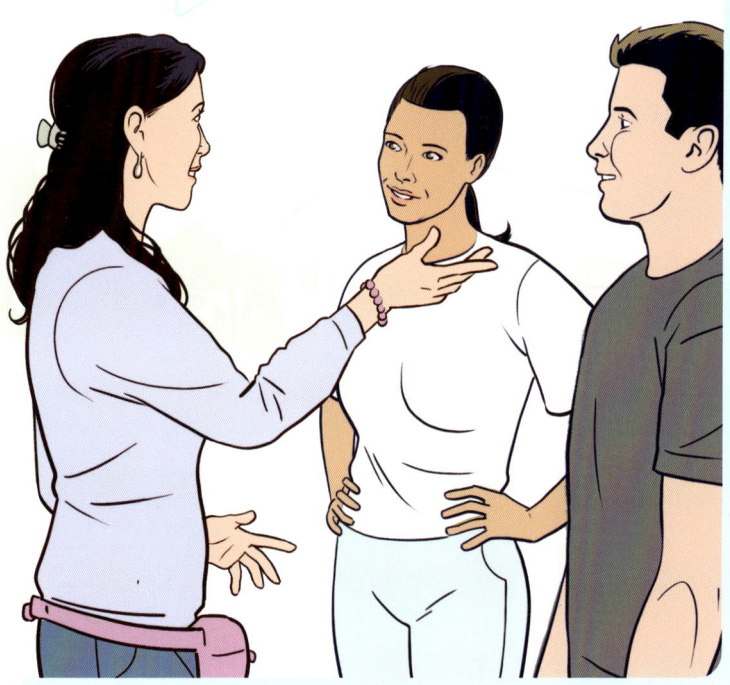

Things That Don't Need To Be Announced

Avoid saying things that are not relevant to anyone in the room, things that you don't know enough information about, or things that no one will know how to respond to.

Other Examples

- I ran into Wendy from next door. She said her son has been getting really into tennis.

- I'm only eating one more cookie. Then I'm done with sweets for the night.

- Remote controls have way too many buttons.

- I'm going to grab my sweater.

QUICK TIP FROM DR. RICK

Unsolicited Parking Help

As a general rule, if it's not your car, it's none of your business. You may think you're a knight in shining armor, but you're actually just some guy in a parking lot waving his arms around. If they needed your help, they would ask. And notice how no one ever asks.

Weather

The calendar on the right represents all the days that weather happens. It also represents all the days when weather shouldn't be your go-to topic of conversation.

SOCIALIZING

ALL THE DAYS WEATHER HAPPENS

JANUARY						
S	M	T	W	T	F	S
					1	2
3	4	5	6	7	8	9
10	11	12	13	14	15	16
17	18	19	20	21	22	23
24	25	26	27	28	29	30
31						

FEBRUARY						
S	M	T	W	T	F	S
	1	2	3	4	5	6
7	8	9	10	11	12	13
14	15	16	17	18	19	20
21	22	23	24	25	26	27
28						

MARCH						
S	M	T	W	T	F	S
	1	2	3	4	5	6
7	8	9	10	11	12	13
14	15	16	17	18	19	20
21	22	23	24	25	26	27
28	29	30	31			

APRIL						
S	M	T	W	T	F	S
				1	2	3
4	5	6	7	8	9	10
11	12	13	14	15	16	17
18	19	20	21	22	23	24
25	26	27	28	29	30	

MAY						
S	M	T	W	T	F	S
						1
2	3	4	5	6	7	8
9	10	11	12	13	14	15
16	17	18	19	20	21	22
23	24	25	26	27	28	29
30	31					

JUNE						
S	M	T	W	T	F	S
		1	2	3	4	5
6	7	8	9	10	11	12
13	14	15	16	17	18	19
20	21	22	23	24	25	26
27	28	29	30			

JULY						
S	M	T	W	T	F	S
				1	2	3
4	5	6	7	8	9	10
11	12	13	14	15	16	17
18	19	20	21	22	23	24
25	26	27	28	29	30	31

AUGUST						
S	M	T	W	T	F	S
1	2	3	4	5	6	7
8	9	10	11	12	13	14
15	16	17	18	19	20	21
22	23	24	25	26	27	28
29	30	31				

SEPTEMBER						
S	M	T	W	T	F	S
			1	2	3	4
5	6	7	8	9	10	11
12	13	14	15	16	17	18
19	20	21	22	23	24	25
26	27	28	29	30		

OCTOBER						
S	M	T	W	T	F	S
					1	2
3	4	5	6	7	8	9
10	11	12	13	14	15	16
17	18	19	20	21	22	23
24	25	26	27	28	29	30
31						

NOVEMBER						
S	M	T	W	T	F	S
	1	2	3	4	5	6
7	8	9	10	11	12	13
14	15	16	17	18	19	20
21	22	23	24	25	26	27
28	29	30				

DECEMBER						
S	M	T	W	T	F	S
			1	2	3	4
5	6	7	8	9	10	11
12	13	14	15	16	17	18
19	20	21	22	23	24	25
26	27	28	29	30	31	

NOTE: If you thought "Hey, free calendar!" when you saw this, it's a good thing you're reading this book.

02

Physicality

Experts say that up to 93% of all communication is nonverbal. Is your body talking like a parent? Find out in the following pages.

A Stance at a Glance

You can dress well and say all the right things, but sometimes just the way you're standing can outshine everything else and signal you've turned into your parents.

Use this guide to know which postures pose the greatest risk of turning you into your parents.

LET'S GET TO WORK

Fig. 1

The Gladiator

Unless you live in the 3rd century and you're posing with a spear, get that hand off your waist and hold your phone like the non-parent you have the potential to be.

THE FIX: Stop doing this immediately. You didn't conquer anything. You're not a statue. Drop your hand. Relax your posture. You're not posing for a painting.

Fig. 2

The Leaning Tower of Dad

If there's a wall or a structure nearby, resist the urge to lean against it. You don't need help standing and neither does that building or pole.

THE FIX: Relax your shoulders. Relax your arms. Relax your legs. Just... relax in general. You're standing, not bracing for impact.

PHYSICALITY

Fig. 3

The Coach

Benches are for sitting, not power-posing.

THE FIX: Put both feet down on the ground where they belong.

PHYSICALITY

Fig. 4

The Lensman

You don't need to engage every single muscle group. The phone weighs 7 ounces, not 70 pounds.

THE FIX: Try using one hand. Try using one finger. Just try using your camera like a non-parent would.

Is a Noise Necessary?

Not all movements warrant a sound. Not everything is an announcement.

PHYSICALITY

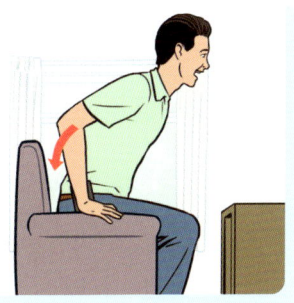
Sitting down

Standing up

Sipping coffee

Yawning

Do not lick your finger
when turning this page.
Or any page in this book.

QUICK TIP

FROM DR. RICK

Nap Traps

"Will people think I'm dead?" is a good question to ask yourself when choosing a place to take a nap. In this section we'll cover some of the more worrisome sleeping locations.

LET'S GET TO WORK

Fig. 1

Park Bench

If they were meant for four hours of REM sleep, they wouldn't be wooden and upright.

Fig. 2

Theater Seating

People are paying for the movie, not for your sleep apnea.

Fig. 3

Restaurant Booths

Unless you're a toddler, there's no excuse for falling asleep during a meal.

Fig. 4

Malls

The benches are for resting from shopping, not resting your eyes.

Fig. 5

Waiting Rooms

The only way to make a waiting room worse, is forcing people to watch you sleep.

PHYSICALITY

Summary

Fig. 1
Park Bench

Fig. 2
Theater Seating

Fig. 3
Restaurant Booths

Fig. 4
Malls

Fig. 5
Waiting Rooms

> Unless you've been hit by a tranquilizer dart, there's never a reason to nap in public. Let's try to keep our sleeping to beds and couches. And to be clear, beds and couches in your own home. A couch in public is not a loophole.

QUICK TIP
FROM DR. RICK

Stretching in Public

There is never a reason to stretch in public. You're a pedestrian, not a professional sprinter. No one is going to randomly challenge you to a 100-yard dash. If for some unfathomable reason you actually do need to stretch, find a private space. No one needs to see that.

03

Clothing & Accessories

You don't need to be a fashionista or a style guru ready for the runway. You just need to not dress like your parents. Let's explore some wardrobe watchouts.

Footwear

A common theme for parents is an obsession with functional footwear. Specialty shoes can be intoxicating and sufferers can often become disoriented and find themselves in strange shoes as a result.

In the following pages you will find the most popular shoe missteps you may have fallen victim to.

LET'S GET TO WORK

CLOTHING & ACCESSORIES

Chunky White Sneakers

Here it is. The flagship of all parental footwear. A tennis shoe on steroids. White, because it's you waving the flag that you've surrendered to *Parentamorphosis*. If you don't know about these already, we've got a long road ahead.

Fig. 1

Fig. 2

Walking Shoes

Remember, it's not a "walking shoe." It's just a shoe. All shoes are for walking. Unless you secretly belong to a "dress shoes only" basketball league, there is never a need for these.

Fig. 3

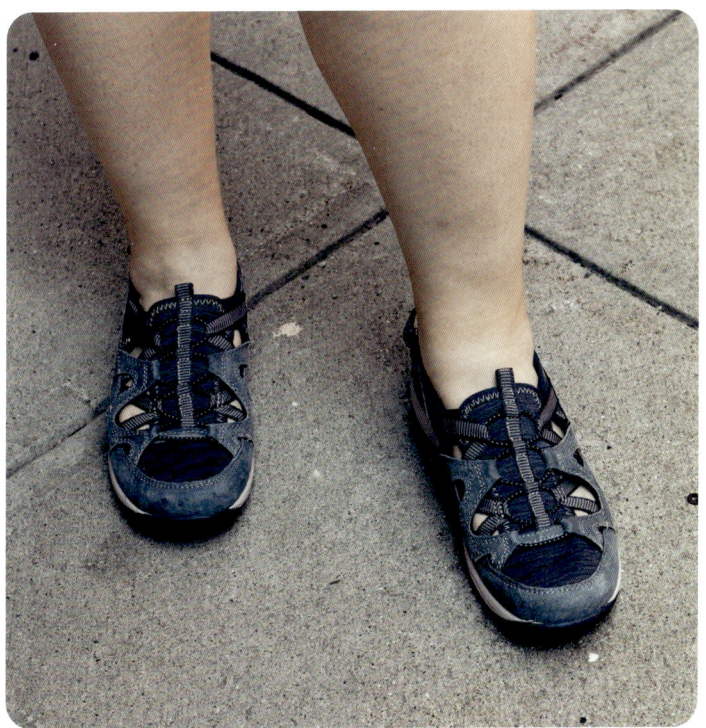

Multifunctional

Waterproof. Breathable. Sandal-like. Unless you're hiding gills and need to switch between land and water at a moment's notice, these are not features you need.

Fig. 4

Chunky Black Sneakers

Unless you're a referee, an umpire, or a ninja with bad arches, there's no reason for you to know this colorway even exists.

CLOTHING & ACCESSORIES

Fig. 5

Sandals with Socks

We should all know this one by now. It's sad it even needs to be included, but it does. It's either too cold for sandals or it isn't. Unless the store you're buying sandals in has complimentary socks for finding your size, this is a hard no.

Fig. 6

Suit and Sneakers

A trap for many commuters turning into their parents. You're walking to the train, not training for a marathon.

CLOTHING & ACCESSORIES

Summary

Fig. 1
Chunky White Sneakers

Fig. 2
Walking Shoes

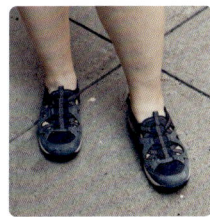

Fig. 3
Multifunctional

Fig. 4
Chunky Black Sneakers

Fig. 5
Sandals with Socks

Fig. 6
Suit and Sneakers

> Beware of how function can overtake form when choosing footwear. It's important to take a step back and reassess...without those shoes on.

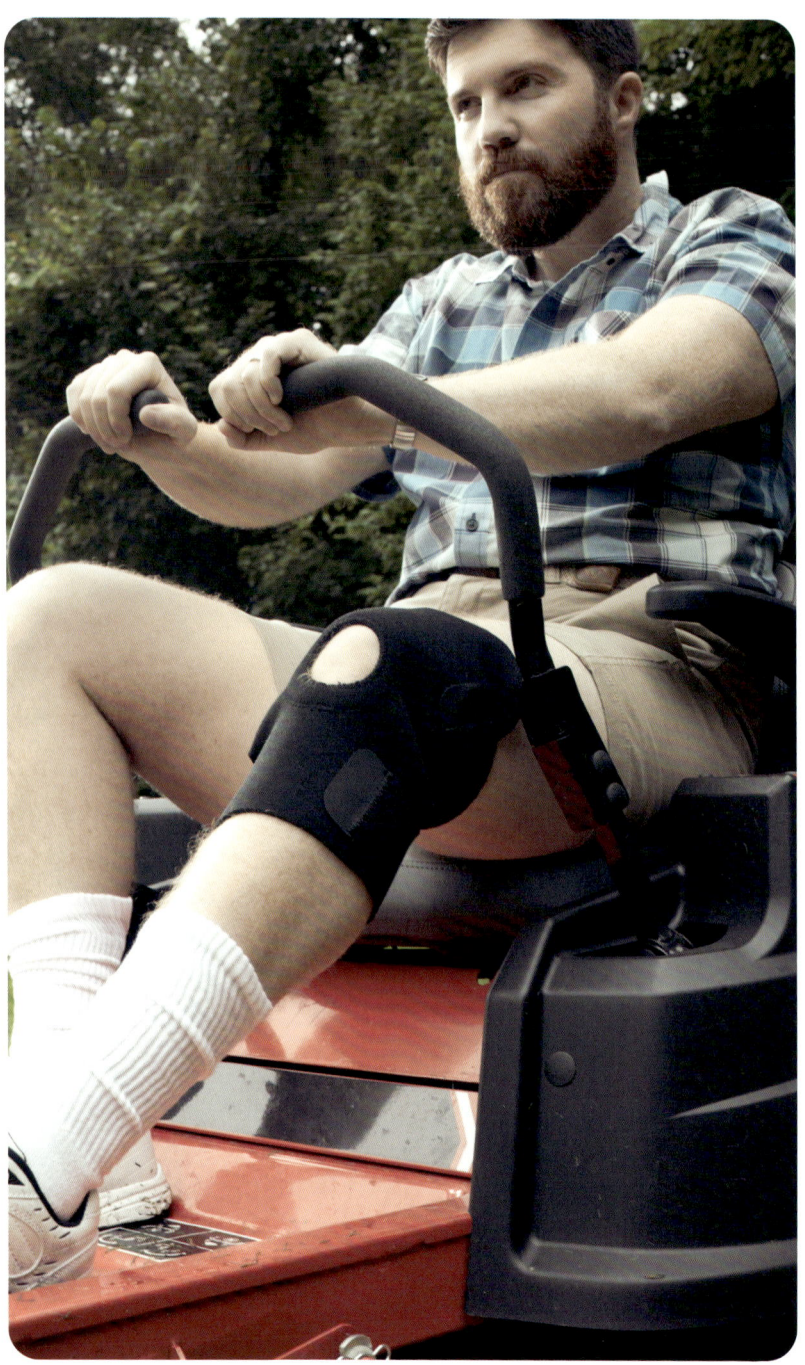

QUICK TIP FROM DR. RICK

A Need for Knee Braces

Unless prescribed by your doctor, there's no need for a knee brace during yardwork. You're not an athlete trying to prevent injury. You're just a person trying to prevent crabgrass. If you're exerting yourself that much, you're doing it wrong.

CLOTHING & ACCESSORIES

Transitioning Away from Transition Lenses

Glasses are worn inside. Sunglasses are worn outside. There is no in-between that requires its own special tint.

Glasses

Don't get stuck in the middle

Sunglasses

QUICK TIP
FROM DR. RICK

Just Because It's Free

Free clothes and hats are tempting. But no one's wardrobe should be made up of swag they got at a booth. Just because "the price is right" doesn't make it right.

Should It Fasten?

Unless you're planning on skydiving or wearing all your clothes at a water park, there's no reason to attach all your accessories to your body. Just because you can strap something to your body, doesn't mean you should.

LET'S GET TO WORK

Fig. 1

Sunglasses

If you're wakeboarding, sure. If you're window-shopping at the hardware store, no.

Fig. 2

Phone Lanyard

It's a phone, not a backstage pass.

Fig. 3

Mobile Phone

Unless you're waiting for an important call while jumping on a trampoline, there's no reason to clip your phone onto your belt. You have pockets for a reason.

Fig. 4

Keys

If you have so many keys that they don't fit in your pocket, you're either a janitor or you need to get rid of some keys.

Fig. 5

Tools

Utility belts are for cape-wearing crime fighters, professional contractors, and officers of the law. Chances are, you're none of those things.

Summary

Fig. 1
Sunglasses

Fig. 2
Phone Lanyard

Fig. 3
Mobile Phone

Fig. 4
Keys

Fig. 5
Tools

> Before fastening something to your body, assess whether you need consistent, immediate access to it, and also whether it might be better suited for your pocket. It is almost certainly better suited for your pocket.

QUICK TIP

FROM DR. RICK

Wind Pants

Pants should be seen, not heard. If you're raising your voice to speak over the swishing of your own pants, you should reassess. The only people who wear wind pants are football coaches and your parents. Odds are you're not a football coach.

04

Home

The home can be a place to relax and unwind. But it can also be the epicenter and catalyst of the worst parental behaviors. Let's take a tour of what to avoid.

Beware of Beige

 Beige is a safety color and an indicator of how far down the parent path you are. If you own more than one item on this list in beige, you're in the right place.

Towels

Vase

Toilet

Throw Pillow

Figurines

Scented Candles

Car

Soap Dispenser

Wheaten Terrier

Candy

Seashell Thing

Paint

HOME

This Is Not Your Glass

So don't touch it. Just because a glass is unattended doesn't mean it's your job to clean it up or put it in the dishwasher. You don't need to ask whose it is or if they're done with it. Because it's not your glass. Pure and simple. And guess what? When you turn the page, this glass will continue to sit here. Maybe for eternity. And you're just going to have to deal with that.

Throw These Things Away, Now

Are you keeping any of these items around just in case you ever need them? You won't. So don't.

HOME

Plastic Containers

Misc. Buttons

Discarded Batteries

Receipts

Old User Manuals

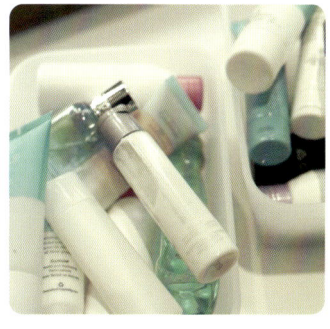

Hotel Shampoos

QUICK TIP FROM DR. RICK

Decorative Soap

Soap is for washing hands, not creating scented seascapes or magical gardens. Shells and flowers don't say you have good taste in interior decorating. They say you are your parents, even in the bathroom. Let's let soap, be soap.

HOME

This Is Not Your Thermostat

This thermostat is none of your business. Just because you come across a thermostat doesn't mean you can touch it, or round it up to an even number, or wonder aloud what its owner's monthly electricity bill might be. It's not an invitation for advice or comment. It is simply a thermostat. And it is not yours. If you had the slightest urge to adjust this, then keep reading.

QUICK TIP

FROM DR. RICK

Aprons Are for Cooking

Aprons were designed to keep food off your clothes, not as a vehicle for terrible jokes and cheesy sayings. Nothing you wear should say to everyone around you "give me a wide berth unless you want to hear knock-knock jokes."

05

Media & Culture

This section will make you think about how your parents approach arts, entertainment, and technology. Then, help you do the opposite.

Holding a Cellphone

While non-parents have integrated cellphone use into their lives in a way that feels intuitive and natural, parents tend to approach cellphones like alien objects, interacting with them in ways that are strange and frankly make no sense.

LET'S GET TO WORK

Fig. 1

Speakerphone

Speakerphone is a useful tool for communicating with groups. However, the entire grocery store is a group that doesn't need to hear you make a dentist appointment.

Fig. 2

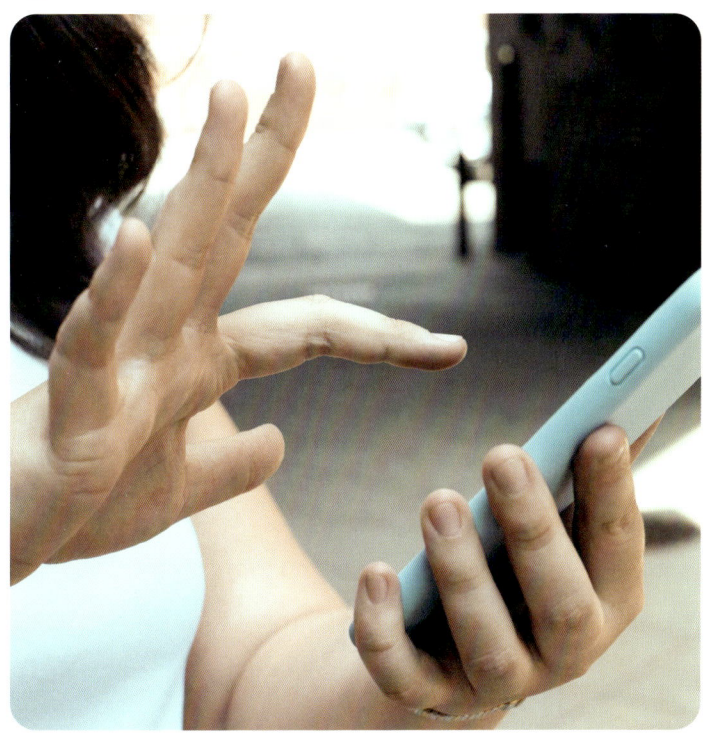

Index Finger

You're using a phone, not an ATM. You have opposable thumbs for a reason.

QUICK TIP

FROM DR. RICK

Tablet Photography

Just because tablets have the ability to take photos doesn't mean they should. There's a much smaller and less awkward option right there in your pocket, purse, or fanny pack. There's no reason to look like you're driving a car with a lunch tray steering wheel.

Watching TV

Watching TV can be enjoyable and relaxing. As long as we avoid a few parental habits.

Blocking the TV

If you can see individual pixels, you're too close. You're watching a BBQ cooking competition, not inspecting brushstrokes on a Renaissance masterpiece. Take a few steps back.

Armchair Announcer

While watching sports, there are people whose job it is to announce what's happening. You're not one of those people.

Familiar Faces

If you see someone you recognize on the TV, you don't need to tell everyone. They're on TV. No one is surprised that you've seen them before.

QUICK TIP

FROM DR. RICK

Passwords

If you were meant to keep your passwords out in the open, passwords wouldn't even be a thing. So let's stop acting like our parents and keep sensitive materials like this more secure than a grocery list or a reminder to water your plants.

Emojis to Avoid

Emojis don't always mean what you think they mean. To be safe, steer clear of all fruits and vegetables.

MEDIA & CULTURE

Looking forward to the farmers market later! 🍆🍅

Read 8:23 am

QUICK TIP

FROM DR. RICK

Plaques

Plaques can be full of great information about historical sites, statues, views, and art pieces. But remember, it's the plaque's job to disseminate that information, not yours. So let's read these in our head, not out loud. If people want to read it, they will.

How to Take a Selfie

 Selfies are generally inadvisable. But if you're going to go through with it, there are a few simple steps you should follow to avoid catastrophe.

MEDIA & CULTURE

Step 1

Take out your phone.

Step 2

Make sure your camera is facing forward.

Step 3

Center yourself in the frame.

Step 4

Press the button.

TIP: You do not need any additional sticks or equipment.

MEDIA & CULTURE

Pronouncing Foods

You don't have to be a culinary expert, but you should be able to make it through an order without sounding like your parents in a foreign country. Here are some of the most common verbally butchered foods by parents.

MEDIA & CULTURE

AÇAI / *ah-sah-EE*

CHIPOTLE / *chi-POHT-lay*

ESPRESSO / *e-SPRES-oh*

FAJITA / *fuh-HEE-tuh*

GYRO / *YEE-roh*

KOMBUCHA / *kawm-BOO-chah*

POKE BOWL / *POH-kay bohl*

QUINOA / *KEEN-wah*

Onward...

You may be done with the book, but the work has just begun. What we covered is only the tip of the parent iceberg. Even I can't write a book that tackles all the dangers of *Parentamorphosis*. But what I can do is leave you with the most important lesson of all...

...You Are Not Your Parents.